We Live in Ireland

Donna Bailey and Anna Sproule

HEINEMANN

Hello! My name is Niall and this is my family.
That's my brother Kevin with our collie dog,
and my sisters Mary and Kathleen.
My little brother Brian is standing in front
of Uncle Seamus, and Grandma's sitting on a chair.

We all live in Ireland.
My Dad is a farmer and our farm is in
County Kerry, in the south-west of Ireland.

Where we live it rains three days out of four.
The rain makes the grass grow well,
and the country always looks very green.
That's why some people call Ireland
the Emerald Isle.

Dad grows wheat and potatoes on the farm.
Irish people enjoy eating potatoes with
their meals.

We all help Dad on the farm, even Grandad.
Grandma gets very cross with Grandad when
he comes inside the house and
forgets to take his boots off!

Mum keeps hens in the yard.
The hens give us all the eggs we need.
Mum sells the extra eggs in the village.

The cows on the farm like the green grass
and give us lots of milk.
We have so many cows that we milk them by machine.
The cows in our picture are going into
the milking parlour.

Inside the milking parlour Dad fits
tubes to the cows' teats.
The tubes suck out the milk from their udders.
Dad plays some music to the cows.
The cows stand still and listen to the music
while they are being milked!

We pour the milk into churns and
I help deliver some of the milk to the village.
Dad takes the rest of the milk to the dairy
where it is made into butter and cream.

Once a month Dad chooses some cows to sell.
He herds the cows down the road to our farm.
Then he loads the cows onto a truck and
takes them to the cattle market in
the nearest town.

On market days you often see cattle
roaming round the streets while
their owners go shopping.

At the cattle market the farmers put
their cows into pens until it is their turn
to sell their cows.

Each cow is led into the ring.
The farmers look at it carefully to see
if they want to buy it.
Then the auctioneer starts the bidding.
The farmer who bids the most money buys the cow.

Grandpa keeps a few sheep in the hills
near the farm.
He keeps the sheep for their meat
and their wool.

Grandpa sells the wool to the weavers who
use it to weave carpets by hand.
Irish weavers also make a cloth called tweed
which people buy to make skirts and jackets.

Grandpa goes to the sheep fair which
takes place every year in Dingle.
He takes some sheep with him to sell.
He likes to meet all his friends and
buy more sheep at the fair.

People in Ireland love horses and
lots of farmers have horses on their farms.
Holiday-makers often stay on farms in Ireland
and go pony-trekking.

The farmers buy and sell horses at different horse fairs like this fair at Connemara.
There are lots of horse fairs
in South West Ireland.

The farmers lead their horses round the ring.
The judges look at the horses carefully
and decide which is the best horse.

At this horse fair in Dingle the farmer
is looking at the horse's legs to make sure
there is nothing wrong with them.
He wants to train the horse to run in races.

With so many horses and fairs
there is always plenty of work for
the blacksmith to do.

Sometimes the farmer sells a mare
and her foal together at a fair.
The buyer hopes the foal will win prizes
at the Royal Dublin Show when it is older.

The Royal Dublin Show is the biggest
horse show of the year in Ireland.
It takes place during a week in August.
Riders come from all over the world
to take part in the show-jumping events.

The show is very popular.
Lots of people go to watch
all the different events.

Before the show starts the band plays
Irish tunes and marches around the arena.

Teams of riders compete in
the different races to win prizes.
This is a relay race where each rider
must pick up a ball from the bucket.

As well as jumping competitions and races
there are other events during the show.
This is a competition to find
the best carthorse.

This is a competition to find
the best horse in the show.
The owners parade their horses
in the ring and the judges decide
which one will be the horse of the year.

The main show jumping event is
the competition for the Aga Khan Cup.
The owner of the winning horse gets
a big gold cup and lots of money.

The riders parade in front
of the grandstand.
Pipers playing bagpipes walk in front
of the horses and the crowd clap and cheer.

Behind the grandstand there are
lots of other things for people to do.
You can even have your face painted
to look like a clown!

Index

HEINEMANN CHILDREN'S REFERENCE
a division of Heinemann Educational Books Ltd
Halley Court, Jordan Hill, Oxford OX2 8EJ

OXFORD LONDON EDINBURGH
MELBOURNE SYDNEY AUCKLAND
MADRID ATHENS BOLOGNA
SINGAPORE IBADAN NAIROBI HARARE
GABORONE KINGSTON PORTSMOUTH NH(USA)

ISBN 0 431 00321 1

British Library Cataloguing in Publication Data
Bailey, Donna
    We live in Ireland.
    1.   Ireland. Social life
    I.   Title   II.   Sproule, Anna   III.   Series
    941.50824

© Heinemann Educational Books Ltd 1990
First published 1990

Editorial consultant: Donna Bailey
Designed by Richard Garratt Design
Picture research by Jennifer Garratt

Photographs:
Cover: Tony Stone Worldwide
Colorific Photo Library: 5 (Martin Rogers), 16 (Ronny
    Jaques), 17, 21 (Linda Bartlett)
Robert Harding Picture Library: 2, 14, 15, 19, 20, 23
    (Desmond Harney)
Royal Dublin Society: 24, 25, 26, 27, 28, 29, 30, 31, 32
The Slide File: 3, 7, 8, 11, 13, 22
The Telgraph Colour Library: 6 (D Kasterine), 9 (Ian
    Murphy)
Tony Stone Worldwide: title page, 4, 10, 12, 18

Printed in Hong Kong

90 91 92 93 94 95 10 9 8 7 6 5 4 3 2 1